101 Things I Learned® in Film School

101 Things I Learned® in Film School

Neil Landau with Matthew Frederick

illustrations by Matthew Frederick

Matthew Frederick is the series creator, editor, and illustrator.

Some of the drawings in this book were modeled after characters and scenes from film and television, under reasonable standards of fair use. They have been included as excellent educational examples of the lessons they accompany. This book is not endorsed by or affiliated with the performers, directors, producers, writers, or other agents of the studios associated with these productions. Readers are encouraged to buy or rent copies of these movies and programs from authorized sources for further education and enjoyment.

Grand Central Publishing
Hachette Book Group
237 Park Avenue
New York, NY 10017
www.HachetteBookGroup.com

Printed in China

First Edition: May 2010
10 9 8 7 6 5

Grand Central Publishing is a division of Hachette Book Group, Inc. The Grand Central Publishing name and logo is a trademark of Hachette Book Group, Inc.

The Hachette Speakers Bureau provides a wide range of authors for speaking events. To find out more, go to www.hachettespeakersbureau.com or call (866) 376-6591.

The publisher is not responsible for websites (or their content) that are not owned by the publisher.

Library of Congress Cataloging-in-Publication Data
Landau, Neil.
    101 things I learned in film school / by Neil Landau with Matthew Frederick.—1st ed.
      p. cm.
    ISBN 978-0-446-55027-7
  1. Motion   pictures. 2. Motion   pictures—Production   and   direction. 3. Motion   picture   authorship.
4. Cinematography. I. Frederick, Matthew. II. Title. III. Title: One hundred and one things I learned in film school.
    PN1994.L295 2010
    808'.066791—dc22

                                                                                          2009037646

From Neil

To my mentors Pamela Long, Carolyn See, and Cynthia Whitcomb,
and to my mother, who taught me the art of survival.

Author's Note

When I graduated from high school, I thought I already knew everything there was to know about movies. But by the end of my first week at UCLA film school, I faced a sobering reality: I was a complete neophyte. Overwhelmed and intimidated by all that was suddenly swirling around me, I wanted to drop out.

Then one of my professors screened and analyzed Roman Polanski's *The Tenant*, shot by shot. It was a tedious exercise, but I was mesmerized. Every frame revealed a theme in Polanski's signature style: paranoia, compulsion, perversity, insanity, obsession, and dark, twisted humor. No detail was random or arbitrary. A pack of Gauloises cigarettes became a symbol of other, more sinister things. Egyptian hieroglyphics on an apartment wall suggested a tomb. The camera's pull toward a window ledge felt increasingly ominous, and creaking floorboards and groaning pipes echoed the cracks in the protagonist's psyche.

If I was partly fearful that such close examination would ruin the spontaneity, entertainment, and mystery of film, I also discovered that it made movies richer and more satisfying. This was the beginning of my deep, abiding appreciation for filmmaking.

In my subsequent twenty years of teaching, screenwriting, and filmmaking, I have been continually struck by how the creative process of filmmaking is at once painstakingly deliberate and fortuitously experimental. From conception through fruition, each project offers unique challenges calling for patience and inspiration, trial and error, talent and fortitude. For film students as overwhelmed as I was and seeking to navigate this process, and for those who simply want to experience films at a more meaningful level, I hope the following 101 lessons provoke and inspire in you a deeper appreciation for the art and craft of filmmaking.

Neil Landau

Acknowledgments

From Neil

Thanks to Hal Ackerman, Alexander Akopov, Jane Anderson, Jon Bernstein, Ross Brown, Walter Klenhard, David Koepp, Allison Liddi-Brown, Denise Mann, Laurie Megery, Gary Ross, Julie Sayres, Richard Walter, Zach Zerries, and Trent Farr for putting up with me 24/7.

From Matt

Thanks to Karen Andrews, David Blaisdell, Sorche Fairbank, Ethan Gilsdorf, Paul Gulino, Jessica Handler, Tracy Martin, Camille O'Garro, Janet Reid, Kallie Shimek, Tim Stout, Flag Tonuzi, Tom Whatley, and Rick Wolff.

101 Things I Learned® in Film School

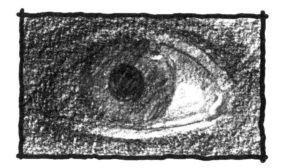

After the opening scene of *Chicago*

Start strong.

The opening image should suggest a movie's central theme and prompt intrigue as to where it is headed. *Working Girl* opens with an aerial shot of the Statue of Liberty, establishing at once its New York City location and the central theme of a woman's independence.

The opening image not only points forward to the theme and story to unfold, it can reveal back-story: An opening shot of a boarded-up, tumbleweed-strewn town may depict desolation, while a flower on a cactus at the edge of the frame suggests the possibility of renewal.

1 I thought I'd find you here.

2 Who let you in?

3 It doesn't matter. We need to talk.

4 You shouldn't have come.

Start late.

A movie story should start as late as possible and occur over the shortest reasonable span of time. A film that uses too much time setting up the ordinary world of the characters or that spreads over three weeks a story that can be told in three days will feel slack.

In individual scenes, don't waste valuable time on unnecessary entrances and hellos. See if a scene can be started in the middle. A screenwriter or director who is willing to self-edit will often find that a scene is strengthened by cutting the first two, and often last two, lines of dialogue.

When Wanda left me, I took it hard and fell off the wagon.

Telling

Showing

Show, don't tell.

Film is primarily a visual medium; almost everything that needs to be communicated about a story and its characters is better shown than explained. Visual cues, when well conceived, will demonstrate the unseen—inner psychology, hidden histories, and emotional conflicts—far better than direct explication will. And if you show it rather than tell it, you will leave more screen time for more important things.

Three stages of filmmaking

Pre-production: all activity prior to the first day of filming, including budgeting, casting, script revisions, location scouting, set construction, creation of the production board (a schedule of when and where each scene will be shot), and hiring of staff and crew. The duration can be many months; *years* may even be required to align everything needed to get a project moving.

Production: begins when the cameras start rolling and ends when principal photography is completed. Lasts from four to twenty or more weeks; big studio movies average about 80 days.

Post-production: begins before production is completed. As scenes are shot, the film editor begins creating a rough version of the movie. Later, visual effects are added and sound editing and musical scoring are performed. Additional dialogue replacement is performed when an actor's line is inaudible or was given an incorrect emphasis. "Post" lasts several months, with the director's first cut usually ready about ten weeks after the last day of shooting.

Filmspeak

honeywagon: on a film set, the trailer housing the toilet rooms

craft services: the snack table

lunch: a meal served to the crew, regardless of the time of day

the day: the time of the shoot, as in, "We'll need a live alligator on the day."

the show: any movie or TV project, e.g., "We worked together on that show."

gimme some love: get me electrical power.

key grip: the head stage hand or rigger on a set

best boy: the second most important grip

gaffer: a lighting technician

check the gate: an instruction to the camera operator to make sure there aren't any slivers of celluloid ("hairs") caught in the opening of the camera. If there's a "hair in the gate," the footage will need to be re-shot.

Abby Singer: the next to last shot of the day

Martini: the last shot of the day

"Revenge"
Project Budget

Category	Est. Cost
Script/rights	500,000
Producers	450,000
Prelim. legal	15,000
Director	250,000
Cast	840,000
Total Above the Line Costs	**$2,055,000**
Production staff	325,000
Art direction	80,000
Set construction	250,000
Set operations	200,000
Permissions/licenses	10,000
Location	50,000
Studio rentals	25,000
Transportation	40,000
Editing/lab	180,000
Music	80,000
Sound	110,000
Insurance/taxes/fees	65,000
Additional legal	25,000
Publicity	100,000
Overhead	100,000
Total Below the Line Costs	**$1,640,000**
Total Prelim. Estimate	**$3,695,000**
15% Contingency	554,250
Total Project Estimate	**$4,249,250**

Above-the-line versus below-the-line costs

Movies are budgeted according to "above-the-line" and "below-the-line" costs.

Above-the-line costs are the "big ticket" items associated with getting a movie into production, including the rights to the script, legal clearances, and the salaries of the director, producer, screenwriter, and actors.

Below-the-line costs are related to physical production: studio rental, set construction and dressing (furniture and props), equipment purchase and rental, location expenses, trucks, work crews, remote living expenses, catering, additional legal fees, music, and editing.

Major studio films invariably spend much more above the line than below.

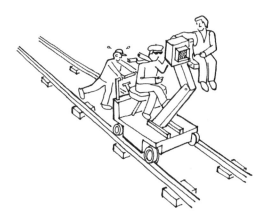

Follow the action.

The camera is the eyes of the audience. Audiences usually want to be as close as possible to the action and not feel like they're observing from the cheap seats. Give them an optimal view by placing, moving, and zooming the camera as needed.

Conceal the action.

Occasionally, curiosity and intrigue are best provoked by keeping the audience a step away from the action. An important conversation filmed through the crack of a door might be more compelling than a full view. A physical attack may be more brutal when heard but not seen. A quirky character referenced frequently but never fully revealed can acquire great, and even mythic, presence.

The *judicious reveal* primes the audience's desire to see and know more, building suspense and leading to a greater impact when a full reveal is later made.

A fixed discovery camera

Discover the action.

Discovery shots selectively show the action while placing the viewer in the midst of a scene.

Moving discovery shots tend to convey a sense of spying, as if the viewer is literally sneaking or looking around the room. Typically, the view begins away from the action, with camera movement gradually revealing the primary action of the scene. For example, a panning camera first shows the empty corner of a bed; then a couple in the throes of passion; and finally a man with a gun in the doorway. A hand-held camera can lend additional immediacy and suspense by suggesting that someone has walked into the scene and is scanning from object to object, trying to decide which details to take in.

Fixed discovery shots lend a sense of eavesdropping, of witnessing the characters' lives from an unobtrusive vantage point within. It uses a stationary camera with the characters moving in and out of the frame; the camera "discovers" the characters from its fixed position.

Make psychology visual.

Change of focus: A character in sharp focus walking into a blurry crowd might be suggestive of an uncertain future. A character walking from a blurred background into a sharp foreground might be getting his values or priorities "in focus."

Low angle camera: A view looking up at a character will make him or her appear powerful. Also known as a "hero shot."

High angle camera: looks down on a character to convey his or her powerlessness or insignificance.

Tilted (Dutch) angle: The horizon is skewed or tilted from horizontal, suggesting that something is amiss or off-balance—physically or psychologically.

Over-the-shoulder: may suggest a character in a vulnerable, ripe-for-attack position.

Jitter/hand-held shot: can project a sense of being overwhelmed while at the center of turmoil, such as a busy emergency room or crime scene.

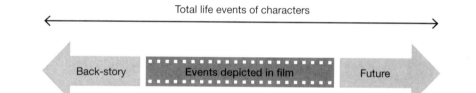

Total life events of characters

Back-story Events depicted in film Future

Control the back-story.

Back-story consists of events that occurred prior to the start of a film: childhood traumas, recent crises, longstanding grudges, the history of the physical setting, and much more. Back-story should be revealed obliquely through casual, but efficient, cues. A woman seen in a Chanel suit at the unemployment office will quickly bring the viewer up to date on a life that recently underwent dramatic change. A character asking "Are you still in love with him?" might tell everything one needs to know about another's romantic history. And a single on-screen event can demonstrate a long-term pattern: A man storms out on his wife in the midst of an argument, and she hurls a high-heeled shoe at him. The shoe hits the door, and a dozen heel marks are seen on the door as it slams shut.

When having difficulty developing or resolving a narrative, look to the back-story, as poor back-story exposition can shadow an entire film.

A flawed protagonist is more compelling than a perfect protagonist.

Inexperienced filmmakers may fail to imbue a protagonist with undesirable traits because they want him or her to appear likable and their cause noble. But a perfect, completely capable hero leads an audience to relax its attention: If he can handle anything, why worry?

Audiences are usually fascinated by contradictions and shortcomings in a film's characters. The idiosyncrasies and failings we all have are even more compelling in a character that is otherwise heroic.

Anthony Hopkins as Hannibal Lecter in
The Silence of the Lambs

13

The antagonist subverts the truth.

A true "hero" has truth on his or her side. Knowing this, the antagonist usually seeks to subvert the truth. Often, the protagonist and antagonist fear the same truth. In a romantic comedy, where the antagonist—the protagonist's romantic interest—is typically friendly, the truth being subverted is a realization or admission of love.

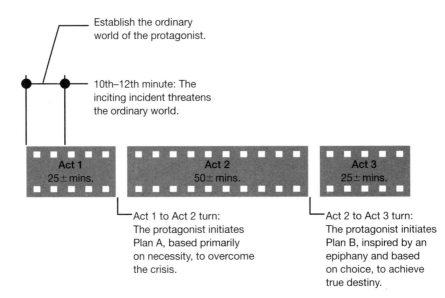

Establish the ordinary world of the protagonist.

10th–12th minute: The inciting incident threatens the ordinary world.

Act 1
25± mins.

Act 2
50± mins.

Act 3
25± mins.

Act 1 to Act 2 turn: The protagonist initiates Plan A, based primarily on necessity, to overcome the crisis.

Act 2 to Act 3 turn: The protagonist initiates Plan B, inspired by an epiphany and based on choice, to achieve true destiny.

Common three-act structure for feature-length American films

14

Beginning, middle, end.

Whether working out the broad concept of a new story, figuring out the particulars of a film during production, or editing a story in post-production, efforts should almost always be directed toward establishing and reinforcing a three-act structure.

Act 1: Establish the problem. Show the *ordinary world* of the protagonist, introduce the inciting incident that disrupts it, and make the stakes clear and compelling should the protagonist fail.

Act 2: Complicate the problem. The conflict grows deeper and broader, and the initial response by the protagonist proves inadequate.

Act 3: Resolve the problem. Events reach their inevitable climax and resolution.

Page number ———————————————————————— 13

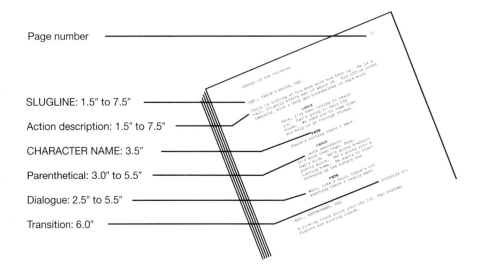

Center of the Universe

INT., CHUCK'S HOUSE, DAY.

SLUGLINE: 1.5″ to 7.5″ ——————— Chuck is sitting at his desk with his feet up. He is a
tall, slightly effete man of about 38. His office looks

Action description: 1.5″ to 7.5″ ——— lawyerly, with a desk and bookshelves of dark wood.

                                        CHUCK
                          Pete, I've been trying to reach
                          you. Dad's going to sell the
                          house. We need you to come down
                          and help us go through things.

                                        PETE
                          There's nothing there I want.

CHARACTER NAME: 3.5″ ——————   CHUCK
                                (with annoyance)
Parenthetical: 3.0″ to 5.5″ ——————— It's more than that. Pete.
                          Dad's going downhill
                          pretty quick. He's going into a
                          nursing home. He wants to start
                          divvying up the estate now.

Dialogue: 2.5″ to 5.5″ ——————   PETE
                          Well, like I said, there's not
                          anything there I really want.

                                                    DISSOLVE TO:

Transition: 6.0″ ————————— EXT., RESTAURANT, DAY.
                          A pick-up truck pulls into the lot. Two shadowy
                          figures are sitting inside.

15

1 screenplay page = 1 minute of screen time.

A screenplay is typically 90 to 120 pages long, which equates with an average movie time of 90 minutes to two hours. Comedy, horror, animated, and family films tend to be on the shorter end of this range because of the audience's more limited attention span and the difficulty of sustaining thrills, chills, and belly laughs for two full hours. Character-based dramas tend to be the longest films, because the revelation of back-story, exploration of inner psychology, and nuances of character development require subtle, protracted exposition.

The more evenly matched the protagonist and
antagonist, the greater the tension between them.

What's at stake?

Show viewers early and clearly what the stakes are—what the protagonist most values in his or her ordinary world and what will be lost if the antagonist prevails. The protagonist's effort to retain the positives of his or her ordinary world while fending off the negative intrusion on it provides the central tension of a movie. When a story lacks tension, it is usually because (a) the stakes were poorly defined; (b) the stakes were not set high enough; or (c) the antagonist is not sufficiently threatening.

Create tangible objects of desire.

A protagonist's goals can be initially abstract, but must become more concrete as the story unfolds. Make goals visual, tangible, and active: proving one's innocence, vanquishing the villain, solving a mystery, acquiring an object or piece of knowledge, producing an event, acquiring an award.

A *MacGuffin*—a term popularized by Alfred Hitchcock—is a specific goal deemed important by the characters early on but that turns out to be irrelevant or worthless to the larger cause.

Practice perfect pitch.

A pitch is a brief summary (ten minutes or less) of a screenplay or film idea, given in person to a film studio executive. When giving a pitch:

1   Have a logline that articulates your movie idea in a single statement. If you can't do this, your idea probably isn't pitch-able.
2   Establish genre, tone, time period, and principal setting.
3   Introduce the protagonist and discuss what makes him or her compelling.
4   Give a lively account of the story's beginning, middle, and end, emphasizing the emotional conflicts. Don't worry about telling everything.
5   If you forget something important, be careful about retracing your steps, as your audience may become more confused than if you had simply moved on. If someone appears confused, ask politely if he or she is still with you.
6   If your screenplay is a comedy, don't say it's funny; *be* funny.
7   If the studio executive is interrupted by a phone call during your pitch, be a good sport. Your first priority is to keep the door open if you don't make a sale this time.
8   End on a provocative high note.

Also prepare an elevator pitch, a twenty to thirty second description of your movie, which will come in handy the day you unexpectedly run into a famous filmmaker.

Not a high concept

A high concept movie can be explained in one sentence.

Selling a movie or TV idea is difficult, but it's far easier when you can articulate its premise in a one sentence logline, for example:

- A billionaire weapons inventor dons an indestructible, high-tech suit of armor to fight terrorists. (*Ironman*)
- A woman has twenty minutes to gather 100,000 Deutschmarks or her boyfriend will be killed. (*Run Lola Run*)
- A man ages backward while his beloved ages forward. (*The Curious Case of Benjamin Button*)
- A curmudgeonly weatherman keeps waking up on the same day. (*Groundhog Day*).

Have a strong *but*.

A clear *but* in a movie's premise is essential to a successful Act 2. For example, "Mamie promises the mob she will deliver a drug shipment from Colombia to Italy, but she's afraid of flying." A premise without a strong *but* will lack sufficient tension, conflict, irony, or humor to carry the middle of the film, while a strong *but* will lead to an Act 2 in which the essential conflict of the film plays out naturally.

With regards to *Seinfeld*

21

A good title says what a movie *is*.

An effective title conveys what a movie is actually about: its central story, the protagonist's quest, the setting, theme, genre—and sometimes all these things. Strong titles are often one or two words that explain a lot (*Speed*, *Jaws*), evoke setting (*Wall Street*, *Fargo*), or suggest danger (*Lethal Weapon*, *Panic Room*). They can provoke intrigue (*The Silence of the Lambs*, *The Curious Case of Benjamin Button*), a sense of risk (*Dressed to Kill*, *Indecent Proposal*), mystery (*What Lies Beneath*, *Suspicion*), and humor (*The 40-Year-Old Virgin*, *Ace Ventura: Pet Detective*). Some are just plain catchy (*Lock, Stock, and Two Smoking Barrels*) or punny (*The Santa Clause*, *Legally Blonde*).

Plot

Story

Plot is physical events; *story* is emotional events.

Plot is what happens in a movie; story is how the characters feel about what happens. In *The Dark Knight*, the plot sets good guy against bad guy, as Batman seeks to protect Gotham City from the deranged Joker. But the story of *The Dark Knight* is the moral crisis Batman faces in risking his reputation for a greater good.

Story

Theme

Story concerns the specific characters in a film; *theme* concerns the universal human condition.

A theme is a truth about life that is embedded in and emerges from the experience of a film. Themes always relate to the struggles and power of the human spirit: honesty is the best policy; love conquers all; one voice makes a difference; be true to who you are; be careful what you wish for.

A film may have more than one theme; in fact, a film's maker and its viewers may differ on which is the essential one.

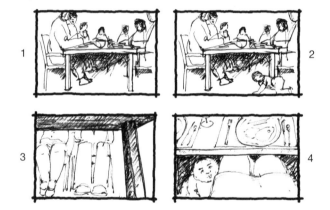

Whose story is it?

A point of view, typically that of the protagonist, presides over a film. POV can also shift within a film: A homeowner peers through a peephole before answering the front door, and we see the caller in a fisheye view; or a crowd of reporters awaits the mayor, and a jittery, hand-held camera places us within the anxious crowd. POV falls into two general categories:

An **objective point of view** portrays events from a neutral, omniscient perspective. It tends to use conventional camera and sound techniques.

A **subjective point of view** portrays events from the perspective of a specific character, with the goal of engendering empathy. Camera angle and height typically replicate what the character sees (e.g., a low camera angle for a person confined to a wheelchair) or feels (blurring or tilting to convey precarious psychology). Variations in sound, color, and light may also be used.

Create memorable entrances.

Your protagonist's character, style, and behavior must be distinctive from the moment we first lay eyes on him or her. Does she trip on a carpet snag? Did she forget to remove a hair curler? Is he carrying a not-quite-concealed weapon? Is he a debonair smoothie amid a hubbub of confusion and crudity? Is she a lone, effervescent figure in a gray London gloom?

26

"An actor entering through the door, you've got nothing. But if he enters through the window, you've got a situation."

—BILLY WILDER

Tell a story at different scales.

A full range of shots (called "coverage") conveys a variety of information and emotions, provides visual interest, lends rhythm and pacing, and gives a director more choices during editing.

Wide Shot (WS; also called Master Shot or Establishing Shot): a broad view that places the action in a physical context the viewer can fully grasp.

Full Shot (FS; also called Long Shot): frames a person from head to toe; frequently used for an entrance, exit, or "walk and talk" (following a character).

Medium Shot (MS): shows a character from the waist up; primarily used for two or three characters in conversation.

Medium Close-up (MCU): shows a character from the shoulders or chest up; used for more intimate conversations.

Close-up (CU): shows a character from the neck up; commonly used to capture one side of an intimate conversation or reveal facial detail.

Extreme Close-up (ECU): shows a character (or object) in great detail, usually the eyes and nose; can show subtext, irony, dishonesty, or detailed activity such as putting on makeup.

Beware the passive protagonist.

Make your protagonist stand for something, not merely against something. He or she can at first be reluctant; an initially fearful protagonist can increase dramatic tension. But the protagonist ultimately must make a clear choice to act; his or her course cannot be chosen for him or her.

After a scene from *Seven*

Props reveal character.

A prop is any object physically handled by an actor, including elements of wardrobe. Props not only make a set more lifelike and believable, but inform on character and back-story.

In *Seven*, Morgan Freeman's character has a metronome beside his bed. Its ticking rhythm comforted him and helped him drift off to sleep. But more significantly, the prop conveyed his desire, as an overworked city police detective, to control one noise in a cacophonous city.

Charlie Chaplin

The human eye can distinctly process about 20 images per second.

At less than 20 frames per second, our eyes try to separately read each image presented to them. In order to suggest continuous motion and not look choppy, a movie must be filmed and projected at a rate greater than 20 fps. The movie industry standard today is 24 fps for film and 30 fps for video.

Slow and fast motion are created by altering the frame rate during filming. Perhaps counterintuitively, slow motion requires filming at a faster rate, and fast motion at a slower rate; a projector operating at normal speed will thereby show the action running at respectively slower and faster speeds. This is why early motion pictures appear to run too fast: They were filmed when a slower rate was the norm, and thereby run too fast on today's projection equipment.

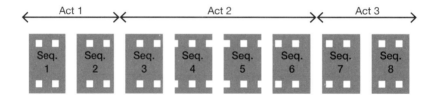

Gulino Model: eight 15-minute sequences

Act 2 is where a poorly structured film goes to die.

31

Because Act 2 is usually twice as long as Acts 1 and 3, it can seem interminable in a poorly conceived film. This problem usually stems from inadequately establishing the back-story or the stakes in Act 1, or not making a clear Act 1 to Act 2 turn.

Theorist Paul Gulino favors an eight-sequence structure to guard against an amorphous Act 2. Each sequence is about fifteen minutes long with its own internal three-act structure. This model doesn't necessarily negate three-act structure, but can be overlaid on it.

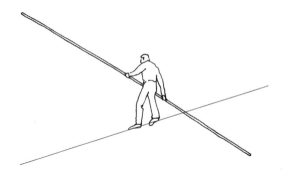

32

The best story structure is invisible.

The audience should never be made consciously aware of structure, which should be camouflaged within dramatic events. When a story is filled with effective emotional stakes, exciting revelation, deepening dilemma, conflict, and suspense, viewers won't try to explicate structure; they'll be riveted to the unfolding narrative.

Every scene must reveal new information.

33

A movie presents a problem; its eventual solution requires that new information be made available to both characters and viewers. Every scene consequently must contain a revelation of previously unknown information. It need not be a bombshell, but should be specific; and if not pure, objective information, it can be about how different characters perceive or react to the same information.

Every scene must contain conflict.

Movies exist because of conflicts and the opportunities for drama, resolution, new understandings, humor, and tragedy. Every scene in a movie—even apparently innocuous ones of blissful courtship or innocent childhood play—needs to contribute to the building and intensifying of conflict. The discord can be modest, overt, embedded in the subtext, sweet, or funny.

In fantasy stories, set the rules early, clearly, and simply.

Fantasy films allow escapism, but that doesn't mean the audience will accept any suppositions they put forth. If the rules of supernatural worlds or powers are not clear, or if new ones are introduced too late, the audience will likely feel that the story they initially invested in has turned into one they are indifferent to.

Animation provides an opportunity to think *expansively*, not expensively.

36

Animation writers can tell any story or have their characters do anything imaginable without the budgetary and physical constraints of live-action movies, in which set construction, special effects, and stunts cost millions of dollars. For this reason, one should be careful about having animated characters do things that can be done in an ordinary, live-action movie, unless it's for humor: If it can be done in real life, why animate it?

Make setting a *character*.

37

Characters might seem the essential objects of a film, portrayed against a neutral backdrop of setting. But setting can have as strong a presence as character. Every setting has unique attributes—climate, topography, lighting, and so on—that influence or are influenced by its inhabitants. Dialect, clothing, notions of personal space, aesthetic sensibilities, and much more can be part of setting.

Because setting is large, one might be inclined to portray it through broad vistas, such as a savannah, beachfront, cityscape, or desert. But details—a rusty fishing vessel, a wizened fisherman, a loon taking flight, a weather-beaten street sign—are crucial, too.

In film noir, everyone is corrupt.

Film noir is a subgenre of the crime/drama/mystery genre. It features opportunistic, morally bankrupt characters full of despair. They act only in self-interest; altruism and playing by the rules are for suckers. There is little hope for these characters, little or no chance for redemption or a happy ending.

The fourth wall

The fourth wall is the imaginary plane separating a stage or film production from the audience. The first three walls are the left, right, and rear boundaries of the stage or set. Breaking the fourth wall means that an actor has consciously acknowledged the camera or audience, thereby violating the distinction between the staged and the real. In traditional film, this distinction is almost always honored, but it is more frequently played with or violated in contemporary and post-modern productions.

Onscreen events and dialogue must be presented with an understanding of their relationship to the fourth wall. If, for example, a character too overtly states the movie's message, the audience will feel that the fourth wall has been uncomfortably broken. Voiceover, in which an off-screen narrator provides insights and information on a film's proceedings, often serves as a gentle negotiation of the fourth wall.

After *The Squid and the Whale*

Dialogue is not real speech.

Dialogue must sound authentic, but it needs to be much more colorful, com-
pact, and on-point than natural speech. Real-life speech is full of asides and non
sequiturs that—unless intended for a specific effect—can be tedious to listen to
in a film. Effective movie dialogue propels the plot forward, informs on character,
and is structured with a beginning, middle, and end—even when the dialogue
begins in the middle of a scene.

Give your characters the anonymity test.

Each character's voice should be distinctive and idiosyncratic. When writing or reviewing a script, cover up the characters' names to see if you can tell who is speaking. If the lines are interchangeable, the characters are too similar.

After a scene from *Road to Perdition*

Mise-en-scène

French for "what's put into the scene," *mise-en-scène* is the sum of factors affecting the visual aesthetic or feel of a shot, scene, or movie, including the interplay of objects, characters, color, depth, shadow, light, shot selection, composition, production design, set decoration, and even the type of film used.

Beware children, animals, and liquids!

- Have double wardrobes for scenes involving foods or liquids.
- Maintain two or three copies of key props.
- Make sure animals can perform the desired actions before bringing them on set.
- When casting children, try to find identical twins or triplets. This will compensate for the unpredictability of children and increase available shooting time, as labor laws and union rules restrict their working hours.
- Avoid extensive sequences involving boats or water, which drive up production costs and make camera movement difficult.

A Steadicam operator

Save time—and money.

Shoot non-chronologically. Use a carefully planned production board with "block" shooting so that all scenes using a given lighting, camera, and sound set-up are filmed before moving on.

Milk the location. With fresh dressing and props or by filming in a new direction, a house's front yard can become a graveyard for another scene, or a coffee shop can become a high-end restaurant. Or, after laying dolly track or building a camera crane, try using the set-up for another sequence, including shooting in the opposite direction.

44

Use a Steadicam. A Steadicam is a special, hand-held camera and harness with technology that evens out jitters. Although expensive to rent (one pays for an operator as well as the equipment), it can provide extensive moving coverage of a scene, saving the time needed to lay dolly track.

Start at the crack of dawn. After sunset, the need for artificial lighting will guarantee additional costs, including the possibility of paying the crew overtime.

Use a second unit. Create a "splinter" camera crew to film wide establishing shots, inserts, and cutaways not requiring the principal actors.

Minimize master shots. If most of a scene is to be presented in close-up, don't burn out the actors by having them sit through multiple takes of wide shots.

Studio or remote?

Scenes are filmed in either a studio (indoor or outdoor set) or remote (real-world) location. The better option is the one that is both cost-effective and faithful to the artistic needs of the story. When deciding between the two, consider:

Cost: It is expensive to transport actors, crew, and equipment to remote locations and house them overnight. But it is also expensive to custom-build a studio set.

Sound: Indoor studios are soundproof, while remote locations are inconvenienced by car horns, passersby, aircraft, and other intrusions that might not be evident the day the location is scouted.

Camera: In a studio set, walls for interior scenes can be "wild"—i.e., movable. This allows flexibility in camera movement that real-world interiors do not.

Permissions: Remote locations may require special permits from the city and clearances from neighbors.

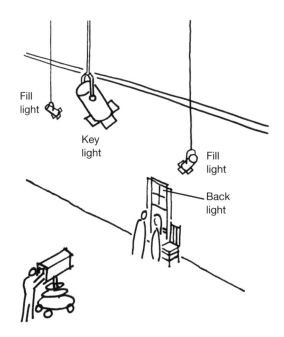

Lighting

A successful lighting philosophy enhances setting, augments character point of view, heightens conflict, and adds visual interest. Lighting choices commonly faced by filmmakers include warm versus cool, artificial (e.g., fluorescent lighting to convey institutional blandness) versus natural (e.g., to lend a documentary feel), the emphasis of side, top, bottom, or back lighting, and the extent of intensity, shadow, and diffuseness.

A key light is the primary light source for a scene. It is usually placed above and to one side of the primary subject. It may be direct or soft or have a color filter.

A fill light decreases contrast, illuminates details in darker areas, and prevents objectionable shadows, such as the nose upon the mouth or one actor upon another.

A back light is placed behind the primary subjects of a scene, facing the camera. It is used to place the subjects in silhouette or provide a glamorous, luminescent, halo effect. It may be softened by a frontal fill light. The sun is a common back light.

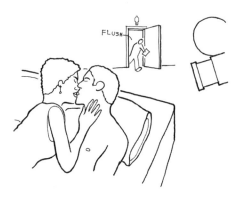

Clear the eye line.

When actors look off camera, considerable clutter may be visible: crew, lighting, sound equipment, more cameras, and much else. For this reason, the assistant director will often say "Clear the eye line" before a take, calling for the removal of all extraneous elements which may distract the actors.

Call "Action" in the mood of the scene.

It takes time and effort for actors to discover and inhabit the desired mood of a scene. If a scene is to be quietly intense, a director can help by whispering "Action" in a soft but firm tone. If a frenetic brawl is to be filmed, he might shout it out like an umpire.

Sometimes the slate clapped at the beginning of a scene presents potential for distraction. The director might call instead for "end sticks," meaning that the slate will be clapped at the end.

Shoot it again.

Even if the first take seems perfect, always shoot one or two more as the actors might offer additional subtleties. Shoot different coverage as well; a variety of shots will maximize choices in the editing room.

Have a plan, but enjoy the detours.

Filmmaking is a complex endeavor calling for detailed plans—story-boards, shot lists, location scouting, rehearsals, and more. It is too complex for even the best conceived plan to hold up the whole way through. So remain fluid. Engage in trial and error. Make room for unexpected interpretations by actors and crew. Turn accidents into possibilities.

50

"All great work is preparing yourself for the accident waiting to happen."

—SIDNEY LUMET

The use of "gak"—foreground elements at the top of
the screen—can help relieve a flat frame (#7).

Signs of a novice filmmaker

1 On-the-nose dialogue in which characters say exactly what they're thinking or feeling in lieu of subtle exposition
2 Excessive use of coincidence
3 Flashbacks that disrupt forward momentum and take the audience out of the moment
4 Voiceovers explaining exactly what can be seen on screen
5 A perfectly good protagonist or perfectly evil antagonist
6 A passive protagonist who does not choose a course of action
7 Flat frames lacking foreground and background enrichment
8 Too many scenes filmed from the same distance
9 Underactive actors who recite lines without seeming to inhabit the scene
10 Uneven lighting
11 Poor sound quality
12 Inattention to continuity, resulting in simple transition errors
13 An ending that doesn't grow naturally or inevitably out of previous events

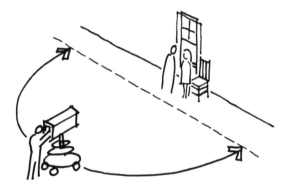

The 180-degree rule

In a given scene, keep the camera(s) on the same side of the actors to preserve the viewer's orientation. Showing the actors from two different sides can lend the erroneous impression that they are not facing in their actual directions. For example, if two characters in face-to-face dialogue are filmed separately and from opposite sides, they may appear as if they are looking away from each other.

The 180-degree rule can be broken for artistic effect, but only with full awareness of the confusion that may be caused.

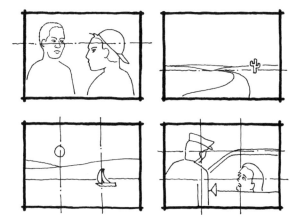

The rule of thirds

Directly centering an object or actor in a frame tends to create a static image that is usually uninteresting and unchallenging to the eye. But by dividing the frame into thirds in both directions, you will have a rough guide for effective placement.

For broad vistas, the horizon line is usually at the lower third. Primary objects are usually best placed at or near an intersection rather than in an open zone. An actor's eyes should usually be near the upper third line.

An exception to the rule of thirds is when conveying a character's isolation or inertia, when a dead-center placement might work best.

Leave breathing room.

Traditional framing seeks to create balance by placing actors and objects comfortably within the frame and giving attention to the spaces around them. Nontraditional framing may be used for artistic reasons—for example, to create an ad hoc, documentary style—but in general, one should avoid making the audience more aware of the camera than the action. Traditional framing is concerned with:

Headroom: Too much space between the top of a character's head and the top of the screen can create an impression that the actor is sinking. Too little headroom emphasizes the chin and neck, and detracts from the eyes—the place we naturally look when seeking the truth.

Lead space (also called look space or nose room): Leave more space in front of an actor than behind. Additional lead space may be needed to frame moving persons to avoid suggesting that they are about to run into the edge of the frame.

Cutoff lines: Avoid framing actors such that the edge of the frame aligns with the body's natural cutoff lines (neck, waist, knees, ankles), in order to not make them appear amputated.

Place figures in uncomfortable proximity.

In Western cultures, the personal space between two persons in face-to-face dialogue is typically over two feet. Onscreen, this distance will usually look too wide, as viewers will become aware of the void in the middle of the frame.

Film is three-dimensional.

It's an easy mistake to limit one's thinking to the literal two-dimensionality of the frame. But inclusion of foreground and background elements—shrubs, fences, hanging lamps, awnings, a porch post—provides spatial and narrative depth for the centrally located action. Even for a straightforward interior scene, it's almost always better to have a window in the background than to film against a blank wall.

Don't create unnecessarily busy backgrounds, however. If two characters are in conversation on a visually chaotic city street, try softening the background focus or have the characters, during an important part of a conversation, pass in front of a screening element. Lighting the foreground while obscuring the background can also help reduce background clutter.

Make sure everyone is making the same movie.

A movie requires not only an artistic vision, but a practical one. Production staff need to get to the set on time, work hard, and take disciplined breaks. Staff can't work at cross purposes, and must always understand the bigger picture into which their work fits. Where interpretation is called for, it must be performed within the context of a larger vision. If this vision has not been explicitly defined, don't assume it's okay to do whatever you want; instead, look for the bigger theme, story, or reason your work answers to.

After a scene from *Big*

Have some showstoppers.

Successful mainstream movies always include several memorable high points, or *set pieces*. These are heightened visual scenes, snippets of which are typically shown in promotional trailers. In a comedy, the set pieces are usually the funniest jokes or squirmiest gags. In action-adventure films, they might show the boldest special effects, chase scenes, or fight sequences. In a horror movie, the set pieces are those that force viewers to cover their eyes.

Every movie is a suspense movie.

Regardless of genre, a film should continually fuel the viewer's desire to "get to the next page" to see how things turn out. As new information and developments are revealed, the protagonist's dilemma should also deepen. Suspense is the product of the interplay between revelation and deepening dilemma: Will the accumulating discoveries and successes be sufficient for the protagonist to overcome her accumulating difficulties? Will the protagonist ever fully grasp the nature of her struggle? Will she resolve it before it destroys her? Will the next scene be the one in which we find out?

60

Random hypothesis

Suspense doesn't come from speeding things up; it comes from slowing things down.

Act 1

Act 2

Act 3

Midpoint (page/minute 50 to 60):
An unexpected curve or
reversal of fortune deepens the
conflict and provokes an
existential dilemma.

Make the conflict existential.

In a complex story, the central conflict should become existential in nature. At the midpoint, make the protagonist's Plan A prove inadequate. Turn the initial crisis into one that is broader, deeper, and darker, and that forces the protagonist to reexamine his or her values and core identity. A memorable conflict not only impels a protagonist to act, but to evolve.

Help the audience keep track of your characters.

Use distinct names. Avoid having an Irma and an Alma, or an Elaine and Eileen, unless confusion is intended. Try names with different numbers of syllables, associating adjectives (e.g., "Silent Bob" in Kevin Smith's films), or using a full name for one character (e.g., "Keyser Söze" in *The Usual Suspects*).

Give characters names that fit perfectly or very imperfectly. One might expect a "Dirk" to be square jawed or a "Mabel" to be old, but you can play with expectations if it strengthens character and story.

Give your characters identifying habits. Pet phrases, verbal tics, unusual clothing, and similar distinctions are helpful, as long as they are not distracting.

Assume the audience forgets details. In a script, restate who a character is if not mentioned in a while. If "CRAIG, 28, the office hunk" is introduced on page 3 but not seen again until page 23, remind the reader with "CRAIG, the office hunk, saunters into the bar." Onscreen, have characters reference other characters by name rather than pronoun when it sounds natural to do so.

Dig deeper.

Good movies are often—or even usually—about simple things explored with depth, nuance, and attention to detail and meaning. Resist the urge to needlessly clutter a film with more and more plot events, hidden agendas, shoot-em-ups, illicit acts, and quirky characters that don't contribute to a central narrative. Instead, dig deeper into the murky gray areas of the events, themes, and emotions already present in the story. Do fewer things, but do them better.

64

M*A*S*H is a rare example of a work that has appeared as
a novel, movie, television series, and stage production.

Film, novel, television, or stage?

Film is best for stories that can be told visually and that demand a satisfying resolution.

Novels are most appropriate when the psychologies of characters are explored in detail, when the writer's prose style is essential to the story's aesthetic experience, and the ending is particularly ambiguous.

Television series suit ideas that can be developed over time. Series involving doctors, police officers, and lawyers are common because the opportunity for new plotlines is virtually unlimited. Serialized dramas (soap operas) offer open-ended plotlines that can run for decades.

Stage plays are suited to complex ideas that can be effectively dramatized via dialogue and a limited number of characters and sets.

65

Tina Fey and Alec Baldwin, after a scene
from *30 Rock* (television series)

Film is a director's medium; television is a writer's medium.

A movie is a one-of-a-kind undertaking: The production team and actors come together for several weeks or months to create a unique world that disappears upon the completion of filming. A strong director is essential in defining this world—from its artistic details to its broad nuances, script approval to casting, set design to special effects, and lighting and equipment to the overall visual style.

A successful television series, by comparison, is long running, and production becomes rather standardized during its first season. The greatest challenge becomes the generation of new material each week, giving the gifted writer a proportionally greater opportunity to shine.

66

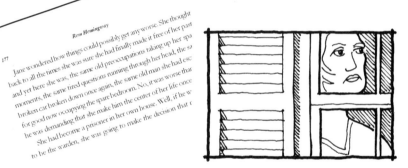

Rem Hemingway

177

Jane wondered how things could possibly get any worse. She thought back to all the times she was sure she had finally made it free of her past and yet here she was, the same old preoccupations taking up her spa and yet here she was, the same old preoccupations taking up her spa moments, the same tired questions running through her head, the sa broken car broken down once again, the same old man she had esc for good now occupying the spare bedroom. No, it was worse than he was demanding that she make him the center of her life once She had become a prisoner in her own house. Well, if he w to be the warden, she was going to make the decision that r

Novel
invisible world
described directly

Movie
invisible world suggested
through subtext

A movie is a novel turned inside out.

A novel directly describes the invisible inner motives and emotions of characters, and leaves it to the reader to formulate a mental picture of the physical world. A movie, conversely, depicts the visible and implies the unseen. Adapting a book to a screenplay thereby calls for a very difficult inversion: The explicit must be made implicit, and the invisible visible.

After a scene from *Harold and Maude*

A comedy isn't just about jokes.

Perhaps no genre offers the clear rewards of comedy, as audience laughter pro-vides immediate proof of success. But the screenwriter or filmmaker who depends solely on gags and one-liners to carry a comedy is unlikely to please an audience for long. A comedy may be experienced at the surface, but it still demands good storytelling, structure, and characters. Good comedy ultimately grows out of its underpinnings—from creating interesting situations and playing with expectations of how they should turn out.

68

Good writing is good rewriting.

A screenplay typically undergoes ten or more full rewrites before it is ready for the marketplace. After finishing a script draft, put it aside for several days or weeks. During that time, give it to several trusted advisors knowledgable in film and writing to get honest, constructive feedback. Then, after revising the draft, find new readers to provide a fresh, objective read. If you use the same readers every time, they, like you, will become enured to the script's strengths and weaknesses.

69

Make rejection a process.

Criticism is inevitable in the arts; it can be difficult not to take it personally. But if a producer hates your movie pitch or script draft, she doesn't hate *you*. In fact, you both share a goal: to get a green light from the studio head.

Consider all criticisms to be inherently valid; there's usually a kernel of truth in each. Even if a critic poorly articulates a criticism or makes weak suggestions for improvement, the fact that he or she is troubled by something you did suggests you should reexamine it rather than expend energy railing against it. And as you try on the suggestions of your critics, more often than not you will come up with a better solution.

When an agent or studio head sends you a rejection, always respond with a thank you note. This may increase the chances that their "no" was a starting point, and that they will want to work with you in the future should you deliver a more viable project.

70

Who is the intersection?

A protagonist typically needs to choose between or reconcile two seemingly irreconcilable situations. A *pivotal character* often provides the crucial connection between the two. It can be a mentor, lover, stranger, marginal relation, or other character who straddles the worlds in conflict. When the protagonist's path intersects with that of the pivotal character, usually in Act 2, the pivotal character provides advice that causes the protagonist to reevaluate his or her understanding of the central dilemma, catalyzing the protagonist's eventual catharsis.

71

Montage

Cinematic montage (French for "putting together") is the juxtaposing, colliding, overlapping, or sequencing of multiple images to evoke deep, holistically grasped meanings. It originated with visionary Russian director Sergei Eisenstein as the idea "that each sequential element is perceived not *next* to the other, but on *top* of the other."

A montage expresses the passage of time and the development of character by economically showing the change of seasons, progression of a relationship, pursuit of a new skill, or physical transformation. Montage is particularly effective in revealing a protagonist's point of reckoning, in which an epiphany is achieved regarding one's priorities, values, and necessary course of action.

After a scene from *The Graduate*

Different lenses tell different stories.

Telephoto and wide angle lenses produce obviously different effects: telephotos (typically 70–1200 mm) narrow the field of view and bring distant things closer, while wide angles (typically 9–28 mm) incorporate a very broad field.

These lenses also have specific effects on movement along the camera's axis of vision. Wide angle lenses tend to exaggerate or accelerate movement to and away from the camera, while a telephoto retards it. For example, an actor moving from the far side of a room toward the camera will appear to move very quickly or abruptly when filmed through a wide angle lens, while an actor moving toward or away from a telephoto lens will appear to be moving more slowly.

We don't always end up where we'd like to be.

We don't always end up where we'd like to be.

Weese don't always ends up where we likes to be.

The plotlines of ensemble movies share a single theme.

Ensemble films feature multiple protagonists with separate plotlines, goals, and stakes. However, the separate stories share a common denominator of *theme*.

One of the protagonists should be somewhat dominant over the others to give the film a center and a point of view. The dominant protagonist is usually the one first encountered in the film, and who gives the film its final punctuation mark.

Make visual motifs specific.

Motifs are visually evocative elements placed strategically throughout a film to amplify theme. They can also act as a structural or pacing device.

Themes are broad and universal to human experience, but motifs should be specific to the story and directly relevant to the experiences of the characters.

75

Rhythm and tempo

Rhythm is the larger pattern created by the duration of the individual scenes in a film. A scene typically lasts from fifteen seconds to around three minutes; the shorter the scenes and the more cuts from scene to scene, the faster a film's rhythm. Rhythm should vary over the course of a film; a movie edited at the same rhythm from start to finish would seem interminable.

Tempo is the pace within a scene. It is determined by the rate of action as well as the number of cuts between views of it. Fast tempos can be exciting, but if overplayed the viewer may tire or become disoriented. A slow tempo gives the audience time to observe nuances of character and absorb the deeper meanings of a story, but if overplayed can provoke impatience.

Rhythm and tempo should be coordinated to create a symphony of counterpoints and complements, with slower and faster pacing playing off each other.

"There's no way on this earth I'm getting on a plane with that man."

"Welcome aboard...our flight time to Harrisburg will be approximately twenty-seven hours..."

Tell the story in the cut.

Good storytelling is often elliptical or oblique in nature; it doesn't always need to show how a character literally gets from A to B to C.

77

Augment action scenes with clean cutaways.

A cutaway is a momentary view away from the main action that provides enriching context or detail. A scene showing a young couple walking on the beach might be complemented with a cutaway of a seagull digging in the sand or an older couple strolling nearby. A scene of a woman engaged in a tense phone conversation might include a cutaway of the sweat on her brow or her chewed fingernails.

A cutaway is "clean" when isolated enough from the general action that it can be inserted during editing without creating continuity problems. For example, an exterior wide shot of two cars careening around a corner can be followed by a clean cutaway of the driver's hand frantically shifting gears, and a return to an exterior view of the vehicles.

Always shoot extra cutaways during filming, particularly for action scenes, to provide more opportunities for improving pacing and dramatic tension during editing.

78

John Williams, composer,
five-time Academy Award winner

The music you hear in your head during filming is probably not the right music for the film.

If you have a "perfect" song or score in mind while writing a script, prepping, or filming, the moment you match it to the edited footage you are likely to be disappointed. The image and the story want what they want, not what you want.

79

After a scene from *Run Lola Run*

Burn your characters' bridges.

It's almost always stronger dramatically to prevent your characters from returning comfortably to their ordinary worlds. Limit their options so they remain trapped in the central dilemma, and their only real course is to keep forging into the unknown.

"I would never write about someone who is not at the end of his rope."

—STANLEY ELKIN

81

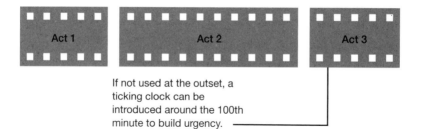

If not used at the outset, a ticking clock can be introduced around the 100th minute to build urgency.

Set the clock ticking.

Give your protagonist a deadline to achieve his or her goal. The deadline can be metaphorical: a general sense that the goal must be attained *or else*. But often the clock can be quite literal and the audience can be made acutely aware that it is ticking.

My Best Friend's Wedding: Can the groom's best friend stop the ceremony before it's too late?

The Fugitive: Can the innocent hero find the real killer of his wife before being apprehended and sent back to prison?

Panic Room: A mother hides her daughter from murderous thieves, but her daughter is a diabetic and in urgent need of insulin.

When Harry Met Sally...: It's New Year's Eve and Harry must find Sally and declare his love for her before midnight, or risk losing her forever.

Read it aloud.

When editing a script, don't rely solely on the voice in your head. Read the script aloud, record it, and play it back to yourself. Or have it read aloud by professional or semi-professional actors, friends, or family. Assign someone to narrate action lines and stage directions so that you, the writer or director, can listen critically. Perform the reading from start to finish without a break so you can hear how and where the story flows and falters.

Afterward, ask for feedback. How did the actors feel about their roles? What rang true and what didn't? Did anyone become confused or bored at any point? Could some things have been left out entirely?

83

Don't cast solely by looks.

Don't assume an auditioner who looks perfect for a role will be perfect. Often the best casting choices are against type, which can help define an iconic character.

Don't necessarily reject a candidate because of an initial bad choice in a reading. After all, he or she won't be directing him- or herself in the film. Instead, give direction to the auditioner and gauge his or her adjustments to it. The auditioner's reaction during an audition is *part* of the audition.

84

Rehearsal isn't just for the actors.

Because a set is usually not available in pre-production, initial rehearsals must be conducted elsewhere. Focus these early efforts on characterization, performance, voice, timing, and chemistry.

When the set becomes available, initiate the process of blocking, by determining the precise movements of actors and cameras. Mark the spots each actor needs to hit with a different color tape on the floor. This will keep the actors from stepping out of the frame, landing out of focus, missing the lighting, or falling beyond the range of the microphone. Save the full dress rehearsal for when you are sure everything has been worked out, which is of course the best way to see what has *not* been worked out.

Give actors something to do.

A director should always give an actor an activity in a scene—ironing clothes, painting toenails, or fixing a carburetor—even if not in the script. The doing should be specific, inform on character, complement or contrast the dialogue, and reveal subtext.

86

Acting speaks louder than words.

People are defined more by what they do than say; indeed, our words often belie our true intent and feelings. Contradictions in human behavior can be used to enhance a story: a strong character with receding body language, an "accommodating" person with her arms folded, and a truth teller who blinks a lot can all gently reveal crucial subtext.

If you want to write, *read*. If you want to make films, *see* films.

The best filmmakers are students of film and literature; their films demonstrate an understanding of, and even make a commentary on, those that have come before. They scrupulously research physical settings, the vocations of their characters, the history of world events surrounding an historical plot, the workings of equipment and props used on set, and more.

Work in the trenches.

Great filmmakers are not born; they are made through years of research, learning, networking, trial and error, and false starts. A good filmmaker is willing to:

Take an acting class. Learning the methods actors use to do what they do will make a more informed filmmaker.

Learn the technology. Cameras, lighting, special effects, editing equipment, and much else change rapidly. The director who stays abreast of technical advances will discover many more opportunities for storytelling.

Learn the business. It is an overworked but nonetheless useful cliché: It is called show *business*, not show *art*. A filmmaker is an artist, but cannot be above negotiating the business and politics of the entertainment world.

Sell. Connections are everything if you have something to offer. Don't be afraid to network and put your ideas out there. Introduce yourself to strangers, even those who don't look like big shots. Getting a big break can take years, and by then a little shot might have become a big shot.

Do unglamorous work. Big breaks can be followed by years of setbacks. Be pragmatic. Some gigs you take to pay the bills, and others to feed your soul. Most fall somewhere in between.

Let it go, already.

Everyone has a script sitting in a drawer that has been waiting for five years for its genius to be recognized. Move on. Genuinely creative people aren't creative once; they constantly come up with new ideas. The masterpiece of a career is rarely the only piece.

Play well with others.

- Relationships formed in film school can last a lifetime. Honor them. Some of your classmates might hire you in the future.
- Have courage and conviction in your artistic vision, but when met with harsh opposition consider that the fault might lie in your inability to effectively convey it.
- Watch your TVC—Thinly Veiled Contempt. Project confidence and competence, but not insecurity or arrogance. Everyone's career is as important to them as yours is to you.
- If you're awful to someone in reacting to their script or rough cut, you increase the chance they will be awful to you when they read or watch yours.
- A director should never be afraid to take a suggestion because of a fear of looking weak. Crews respect a director who is open to suggestions, and will work more happily—and harder—for him or her.

Make it shorter.

No matter how clever or insightful you think a scene, setting, camera angle, or line of dialogue, subject it to deep scrutiny. Is it absolutely necessary to the story? Does it prepare the audience for what comes next? Does it reveal and deepen character? If you are unsure, it probably isn't needed.

Ultimately, everything must serve to advance the plot and inform on character. Words and actions that do not serve these ends, not matter how clever, funny, or insightful, should usually be excised.

"Perfection is achieved, not when there is nothing more to add, but when there is nothing left to take away."

—ANTOINE DE SAINT-EXUPÉRY

93

Convenient versus inconvenient coincidences

Make your protagonist earn every triumph and piece of information; don't use plot conveniences like eavesdropping or accidental discovery of crucial data to help the protagonist solve his or her dilemma. If you do introduce a coincidence, it will be more acceptable to the audience if it makes the protagonist's quest more difficult rather than easier.

94

Hang a lantern.

Resolving a complex story in two hours is difficult; the introduction of plot contrivances may at times seem unavoidable. A way out of this problem is to "hang a lantern"—to have an on-screen character question the same logic an audience is likely to question. When a character is willing to acknowledge the improbable, the audience may be more willing to go along with it.

Don't overtax an audience's good will.

Audiences go to movies to be entertained—to laugh, cry, or even be afraid—and will usually accept cheerfully an initial contrivance or extreme coincidence to get a story going. However, their "willing suspension of disbelief" can easily evaporate if they are asked to accept too many contrivances. They will roll their eyes at too much cliché and predictability, groan at excessive coincidences, and heckle when the ingénue goes down to the dark basement to investigate an intruder. When taken out of the moment, an audience will often find that the actor's fame eclipses his or her believability as a character.

96

Deus ex machina

In less successful examples of classical Greek theatre, an intractable problem was sometimes resolved by the appearance of a god via a mechanical armature or other device. *Deus ex machina*—literally, "god from the machine"—has since come to refer to any plot contrivance that miraculously emerges to resolve an intractable dilemma. It invariably disappoints viewers, who prefer to see a character in whom they are invested become empowered to solve his or her own problem.

After a scene from *A Few Good Men*

The climax is the *truth*.

A climax is more than the point of highest action or plot revelation; it is the moment at which the protagonist recognizes his or her existential core. The protagonist's false self, previously supported by secrets, lies, shame, or fear, may be stripped away so that a truer, more fulfilled self may emerge.

A hero accepts and evolves in the face of the truth, except in a tragedy, where the protagonist's inability to evolve leads to a tragic outcome.

After the climax, get out fast.

After the plot reaches its climax, there are few places for a film to go that won't feel superfluous. Resolve the plot and primary subplots satisfyingly, but don't feel obligated to tie up every loose end. Leave the audience wanting more. Often, a *suggestion* of how the characters end up is more powerful than showing exactly how they *do* end up. Nonetheless, when creating an ambiguous ending, have a clear point-of-view with which the viewer may agree or disagree.

Catharsis

Upon the climax and denouement, the characters and audience should undergo *catharsis*, an emotional release that Aristotle defined as "the purging or cleansing of pity and fear." It may also evoke sadness, anger, sorrow, laughter, or other emotional responses; ultimately catharsis serves to restore or re-center one's emotions or understanding. It is virtually impossible for an audience to experience catharsis unless the protagonist faces and releases his or her greatest fear.

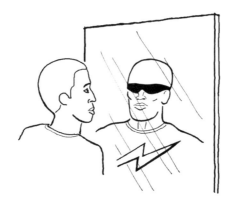

You are your protagonist.

A film may be viewed by millions, but filmmaking is ultimately a personal endeavor that directly draws from and touches the life of a filmmaker. We create stories to mirror our own lives, to see how we will react when projected into the extraordinary circumstances of a film story. This is a major reason why it is difficult to create a flawed protagonist: A storyteller must publicly display him-or herself as flawed.

Telling the story you are most afraid to tell—taking real, personal risks, dramatizing taboo events, pushing the protagonist to the edge of reason, showing things that seem too confrontational or emotionally raw for the audience—is most likely to translate into a provocative, memorable film experience.

Neil Landau is a screenwriter whose television and film credits include *Don't Tell Mom the Babysitter's Dead*, *Melrose Place*, *Doogie Howser, M.D.*, *The Magnificent Seven*, and *Twice in a Lifetime*. He has developed feature films for 20th Century Fox, Disney, Universal, and Columbia Pictures, and television pilots for Warner Bros., Touchstone, Lifetime, and CBS. He works internationally as a script consultant and teaches at UCLA's School of Film, Television, and Digital Media. He lives in Los Angeles.

Matthew Frederick is an architect, urban designer, teacher, author of the bestselling *101 Things I Learned in Architecture School*, and the creator, editor, and illustrator of the 101 Things I Learned series. He lives in Cambridge, Massachusetts.